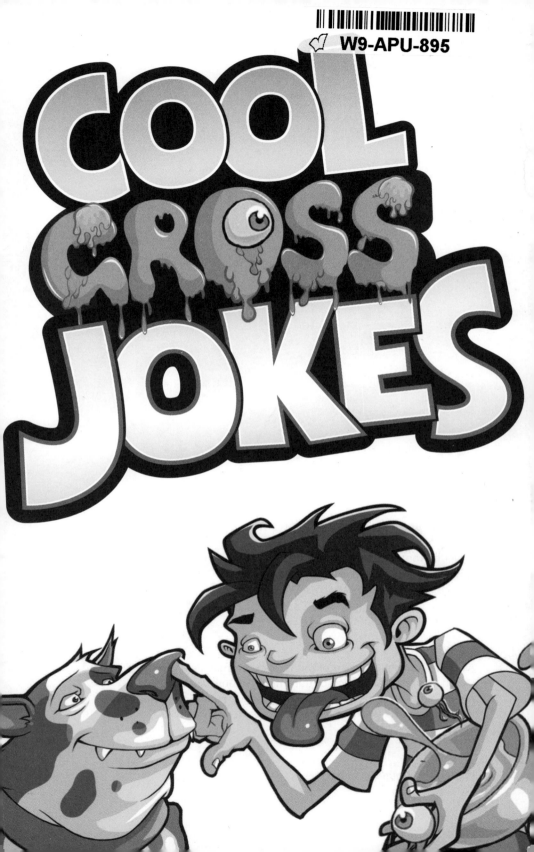

COOL CROSS JOKES

Published by Hinkler Books Pty Ltd 2015
45–55 Fairchild Street
Heatherton Victoria 3202 Australia
www.hinkler.com.au

© Hinkler Books Pty Ltd 2004, 2010, 2014, 2015

Cover design: Hinkler Books Studio
Cover illustration and illustrations: Rob Kiely
Joke collection: Nicolas Brasch and Barb Whiter
Prepress: Graphic Print Group
Typesetting: MPS Limited

ISBN: 978 1 4889 2627 3

Printed and bound in China

CONTENTS

Riddles, Riddles, Riddles

1 **W**hat's green, sticky and smells like eucalyptus?
Koala vomit.

2 **W**hat do termites eat for dessert?
Toothpicks.

3 **W**hy did Piglet look in the toilet?
He was looking for Pooh.

4 **W**hy do little brothers chew with their mouths full?

Flies have to live somewhere.

5 **W**hat do you get if you sit under a cow?

A flat head.

6 **M**ummy, Mummy, can I lick the bowl?

No! You'll have to flush like everyone else.

7 **W**hat's the difference between a maggot and a cockroach?

Cockroaches crunch more when you eat them.

8 **W**hy do elephants have trunks?

Because they can't fit everything into a handbag.

9   **W**hat's brown and sounds like a bell?

Dung.

10   **W**hy do petrol stations always lock their toilets?

They are afraid someone might clean them.

11   **W**hat do you do if your nose goes on strike?

Picket.

12   **H**ow does a monster count to thirteen?

On his fingers.

13   **H**ow can you tell when a moth farts?

He flies straight for a second.

14   **H**ow do you make a tissue dance?

Put some boogie into it.

15   **W**hat has two grey legs and two brown legs?

An elephant with diarrhoea.

16 **W**hy did your sister put her socks on inside out?

Because there was a hole on the outside.

17 **W**hat's another name for a snail?

A booger with a crash helmet.

18 **W**hat's yellow and smells of bananas?

Monkey vomit.

19 **W**hat's green and red and goes at 120 km/h?

A frog in a blender.

20 **W**hat has fifty legs and can't walk?

Half a centipede.

21 What's the difference between school lunches and a pile of slugs?

School lunches are on plates.

22 What do sea monsters eat?

Fish and ships.

23 What did the royal taster say after drinking the poisoned water?

Not much!

24 **W**hat do you get when you cross a vampire with a dwarf?

A monster that sucks blood out of people's kneecaps.

25 **W**hich area of the police force accepts monkeys?

The Special Branch.

26 **D**id you hear the joke about the fart?

It stinks.

27 **W**hat did the first mate see in the toilet?

The captain's log.

28 **W**hy do hot dogs have such bad manners?
They spit in the frying pan.

29 **W**hat is black and white, and red all over?
A nun in a blender.

30 **W**hat's green and slimy, and hangs from trees?
Giraffe boogers.

31 **W**hy wasn't the butterfly invited to the dance?

Because it was a moth ball.

32 **W**hat's green, has two legs, and sits on the end of your finger?

The boogeyman.

Poking Fun at Teachers

33 **S**cience teacher: *'What are nitrates?'*

Student: *'Cheaper than day rates.'*

34 **E**nglish teacher: *'Jamie, give me a sentence beginning with "I".*

Jamie: *'I is ...'.*

Teacher: *'No Jamie, you must always say "I am".'*

Jamie: *'Okay. I am the ninth letter of the alphabet.'*

35 **H**istory teacher: *'What's a Grecian urn?'*

Student: *'About $500 a week.'*

36 **W**hat's the difference between a train station and a teacher?

One minds the train, the other trains the mind.

37 **D**id you hear about the maths teacher who wanted to order pizza for dinner, but was divided about whether to have additional cheese?

Here's your ·74 share of the entire pizza with 0·25% extra cheese!

38 **T**eacher: *'Did you know the bell had gone?'*
Sue: *'I didn't take it, Miss.'*

39 **H**istory teacher: *'What was Camelot?'*
Student: *'A place where camels are parked.'*

40 **T**eacher: *'If I bought 100 buns for a dollar, what would each bun be?'*
Student: *'Stale.'*

One of those stale old bargain buns that made its way into the teacher's lunchbox

41 **T**eacher: *'Wally, why are you late?'*
Wally: *'The train had a flat tyre.'*

42 **H**istory teacher: *'What's the best thing about history?'*
Mary: *'All the dates.'*

43 In which class do you learn how to shop for bargains?

Buy-ology.

44 '**M**ary,' said her teacher. *'You can't bring that lamb into class. What about the smell?'*

'Oh, that's all right Miss,' replied Mary. *'It'll soon get used to it.'*

45 '**W**hat are three words most often used by students?' the teacher asked the class.

'I don't know,' sighed a student.

'That's correct!' said the teacher.

46 **S**hane: *'Dad, today my teacher yelled at me for something I didn't do.'*

Dad: *'What did he yell at you for?'*

Shane: *'For not doing my homework.'*

47 **W**hen George left school he was going to be a printer.

All his teachers said he was the right type.

48 **T**eacher: *'What came after the Stone Age and the Bronze Age?'*

Student: *'The saus-age.'*

49 **P**rincipal: *'You should have been here at 9.00.'*
Student: *'Why, what happened?'*

50 **M**other: *'Did you get a good place in the geography test?'*
Daughter: *'Yes, I sat next to the cleverest kid in the class.'*

51 **T**eacher: *'That's three times I've asked you a question. Why won't you reply?'*
Student: *'Because you told me not to answer you back.'*

52 **G**eography teacher: *'What's the coldest country in the world?'*
Student: *'Chile.'*

53 **H**ow many aerobic teachers does it take to change a light bulb?
Five, one to change it, the others to say, 'A Little to the left, a little to the right, a little to the left, a little to the right.'

54 History teacher: *'Here is a question to check that you did your homework on British kings and queens. Who came after Mary?'*

Student: *'Her little lamb.'*

55 History teacher: *'Why do we refer to the period around 1000 years AD as the Dark Ages?'*

Student: *'Because there were so many knights.'*

56 When Dad came home, he was amazed to see his son sitting on a horse, writing something. *'What are you doing up there?'* he asked.

'Well, the teacher told us to write an essay on our favourite animal,' replied the boy.

57 Why did the teacher wear sunglasses?

Because his students were so bright.

58 Cookery teacher: *'Helen, what are the best things to put in a fruit cake?'*

Helen: *'Teeth!'*

59 **D**id you hear about the cross-eyed teacher?

He couldn't control his pupils.

60 **F**ather: *'I want to take my girl out of this terrible maths class.'*

Teacher: *'But she's top of the class!'*

Father: *'That's why it must be a terrible class!'*

61 **T**eacher: *'I'd like you to be very quiet today, girls. I've got a dreadful headache.'*

Mary: *'Please Miss, why don't you do what Mum does when she has a headache?'*

Teacher: *'What's that?'*

Mary: *'She sends us out to play!'*

62 **M**aths teacher: *'Paul. If you had five pieces of chocolate and Sam asked for one of them, how many would you have left?'*

Paul: *'Five.'*

63 **T**eacher: *'I hope I didn't see you copying from John's exam paper, James.'*

James: *'I hope you didn't see me either!'*

64 **W**hat is the robot teacher's favourite part of the day?

Assembly.

65 **W**hat is the easiest way to get a day off school?

Wait until Saturday.

66 **S**cience teacher: *'Which travels faster, heat or cold?'*

Student: *'Heat, because you can catch a cold.'*

67 **W**hat would you get if you crossed a teacher with a vampire?

Lots of blood tests.

68 **S**tudent to teacher: *'I don't want to worry you but my dad said that if my grades don't improve, someone's going to get a spanking.'*

69 **T**eacher: *'What's the name of a liquid that won't freeze?'*
Student: *'Hot water.'*

70 **T**eacher: *'Can anyone tell me what the Dog Star is?'*
Student: *'Lassie.'*

71 **T**eacher: *'I wish you'd pay a little attention.'*

Student: *'I'm paying as little attention as possible.'*

72 **S**tudent: *'Would you punish someone for something they didn't do?'*

Teacher: *'Of course not.'*

Student: *'Good, because I didn't do my homework.'*

73 **T**eacher: *'Billy, stop making ugly faces at the other students!'*

Billy: *'Why?'*

Teacher: *'Well, when I was your age, I was told that if I kept making ugly faces, my face would stay that way.'*

Billy: *'Well, I can see you didn't listen.'*

74 Have you heard about the gym teacher who ran around exam rooms, hoping to jog students' memories?

75 ... Or, the craft teacher who had her pupils in stitches?

76 ... Or, maybe, the cookery teacher who thought Hamlet was an omelette with bacon?

77 Dad: *'How did you find your maths exam?'*
Son: *'Unfortunately, it wasn't lost!'*

78 What is an English teacher's favourite fruit?
The Grapes of Wrath.

LOST CHILD

HAVE YOU SEEN HIM?

Someone should recognise the little guy. He's got 8 legs.

79 Teacher: *'Why can't you answer any of my questions in class?'*
Student: *'If I could, there wouldn't be much point in me being here.'*

80 Teacher: *'What family does the octopus belong to?'*
Student: *'Nobody's I know.'*

81 Why can you believe everything a bearded teacher tells you?
They can't tell bare-faced lies.

82 **D**id you hear about the two history teachers who were dating?

They go to restaurants to talk about old times.

83 **W**hy are maths teachers good at solving detective stories?

Because they know when all the clues add up.

84 **W**hat do you call a teacher with a school on his head?

Ed.

85 **T**eacher to parent: *'David's career choice as a train driver will suit him well. He has more experience of lines than any other student at this school!'*

86 First teacher: *'What's wrong with young Jimmy today? I saw him running around the playground, screaming and pulling at his hair.'*

Second teacher: *'Don't worry. He's just lost his marbles.'*

87 What word is always spelled wrong?

Wrong.

88 Maths teacher: *'Anne, why have you brought a picture of the queen of England with you today?'*

Anne: *'You told us to bring a ruler with us.'*

89 Maths teacher: *'Richard, if you had 50 cents in each trouser pocket, and $2 in each blazer pocket, what would you have?'*

Richard: *'Someone else's uniform, Sir.'*

90 What kind of tests do witch teachers give?

Hex-aminations.

91 Student: *'I don't think I deserve a zero on this test.'*

Teacher: *'No, neither do I but it was the lowest I could give you!'*

92 **T**eacher: *'Jessica, you aren't paying attention to me. Are you having trouble hearing?'*

Jessica: *'No, I'm having trouble listening.'*

93 **M**aths teacher: *'If you multiplied 1386 by 395, what would you get?'*

Student: *'The wrong answer.'*

94 **T**eacher: *'You missed school yesterday, didn't you?'*

Student: *'Not very much.'*

95 **'O**ur teacher talks to herself in class, does yours?'

'Yes, but she doesn't realise it. She thinks we're listening!'

96 **P**laying truant from school is like having a credit card.

Lots of fun now, pay later.

97 **L**augh, and the class laughs with you.

But you get detention alone.

98 **S**tudent: *'I didn't do my homework because I lost my memory.'*

Teacher: *'When did this start?'*

Student: *'When did what start?'*

99 **W**hy was the head teacher worried?

Because there were so many rulers in the school.

100 **T**eacher: *'I told you to stand at the end of the line.'*

Student: *'I tried, but there was someone already there.'*

101 **T**eacher: *'Why didn't you answer me, Stuart?'*

Stuart: *'I did, I shook my head.'*

Teacher: *'You don't expect me to hear it rattling from here, do you?'*

102 **T**eacher: *'I said to draw a cow eating grass, but you've only drawn a cow.'*

Student: *'Yes, the cow has eaten all the grass.'*

103 **D**id you hear about the teacher who locked the school band in a deep freeze?

They wanted to play really cool jazz.

104 **T**eacher: *'Why haven't you been to school for the last two weeks, Billy?'*

Billy: *'It's not my fault – whenever I go to cross the road outside, there's a man with a sign saying '"Stop Children Crossing"'!'*

105 **D**id you hear about the teacher who wore sunglasses to give out exam results?

He took a dim view of his students' performance.

106 **H**istory teacher: *'Why were ancient sailing ships so eco-friendly?'*

Student: *'Because they could go for hundreds of miles to the galleon.'*

107 Teacher: *'What's the name of a bird that doesn't build its own nest?'*

Student: *'The cuckoo.'*

Teacher: *'That's right – how did you know that?'*

Student: *'Easy, Sir, everyone knows cuckoos live in clocks!'*

108 How does a maths teacher know how long she sleeps?

She takes a ruler to bed.

109 Did you hear about the technology teacher who left teaching to try to make something of himself?

110 Why did the boy throw his watch out of the window during an exam?

Because he wanted to make time fly.

111 English teacher: *'James, give me a sentence with the word "counterfeit" in it.'*

James: *'I wasn't sure if she was a centipede or a millipede, so I had to count her feet.'*

112 Computer teacher: *'Sarah, give me an example of software.'*

Sarah: *'A floppy hat.'*

113 '**W**hat were you before you came to school, girls and boys?' asked the teacher, hoping that someone would say 'babies'. She was disappointed when all the children cried out, 'Happy!'

114 **S**tudent 1: 'We bought our retiring science teacher a gift – toilet water that cost $20.'

Student 2: 'What! I would've sold you water from our toilets for only $2!'

115 **T**eacher: 'That's the stupidest boy in the whole school.'

Mother: 'That's my son.'

Teacher: 'Oh! I'm so sorry.'

Mother: 'You're sorry!'

116 '**I** hope you're not one of those boys who sits and watches the school clock,' said the principal to the new boy.

'No, Sir,' he replied. 'I've got a digital watch that beeps at three-fifteen!'

117 **T**eacher: 'Your daughter's only five and she can spell her name backwards! Why, that's remarkable!'

Mother: 'Yes, we're very proud of her.'

Teacher: 'And what is your daughter's name?'

Mother: 'Anna.'

118 *'**H**ow old would you say I am, Francis?'* the teacher asked.

'Forty,' said the boy promptly.

'What makes you think I'm forty?' asked the puzzled teacher.

'My big brother is twenty,' he replied, *'and you're twice as silly as he is!'*

119 **M**y teacher says I've got such bad handwriting that I ought to be a doctor!

120 *'**D**o you like your new school, Billy?'* asked Uncle Ned.

'Sometimes,' said the boy.

'When is that?'

'When it's closed!'

121 **B**en's teacher thinks Ben is a wonder child.

She wonders whether he'll ever learn anything.

122 *'**I**'m not going to school today,'* said Alexander to his mother. *'The teachers bully me and the boys in my class don't like me. Why?'*

'Firstly, you're 35 years old,' replied his mother, *'and secondly, you're the principal!'*

123 **S**imple Simon was writing a geography essay for his teacher. It began like this: *The people who live in Paris are called parasites.*

124 **T**eacher: *'Are you good at arithmetic?'*
Mary: *'Well, yes and no.'*
Teacher: *'What do you mean, yes and no?'*
Mary: *'Yes, I'm no good at arithmetic.'*

125 **T**eacher: *'If you had one dollar and asked your dad for one dollar, how much money would you have?'*

Student: *'One dollar.'*

Teacher: *'You don't know your maths.'*

Student: *'You don't know my dad!'*

126 **'B**e sure to go straight home from school.'

'I can't – I live around the corner!'

Animal Crackers

127 **W**hat time is it when an elephant climbs into your bed?

Time to get a new bed.

128 **W**hat do you get if you pour hot water down a rabbit hole?

Hot cross bunnies.

129 **W**hy do buffaloes always travel in herds?

Because they're afraid of getting mugged by elephants.

130 **W**hat do you give a sick elephant?

A very big paper bag.

131 **W**here do elephants go on holidays?
Tuscany.

132 **W**hy are elephants big and grey?
Because if they were small and purple they would be grapes.

133 **W**hat do you call the red stuff between an elephant's toes?
A slow explorer.

134 **W**hy do elephants have Big Ears?
Because Noddy wouldn't pay the ransom.

135 **W**hat do you call an amorous insect?
The love bug!

136 **W**here would you find a dog with no legs?
Exactly where you left it.

137 **W**hat did the buffalo say to his son, when he went away on a long trip?
'Bison.'

138 '**D**oes your dog bite?'

'No.'

'Oww. I thought you said your dog doesn't bite.'

'That's not my dog.'

139 **N**ame an animal that lives in Lapland.

A reindeer.

Now name another.

Another reindeer.

140 **W**hat sits in the middle of the World Wide Web?

A very, very big spider.

141 **D**id you hear about the duck who bought some lipstick?

She asked the chemist to put it on her bill.

142 **C**ow 1: 'Are you concerned about catching mad cow disease?'

Cow 2: 'Not at all. I'm a sheep.'

143 **D**id you hear about the acrobatic snake?

He was in Monty Python's Flying Circus.

144 **H**ow did the frog die?

It Kermit-ted suicide.

145 **D**o you know where to find elephants?

Elephants don't need finding – they're so big they don't get lost.

146 **D**id you hear about the cannibal lioness?

She swallowed her pride.

147 **W**hat is a polygon?

A dead parrot.

148 **W**hat's the difference between a mouse and an elephant?

About a tonne.

149 **W**hat did the lioness say to the cub chasing the hunter?

Stop playing with your food.

150 **W**hat do you get when you cross a master criminal with a fish?

The Codfather.

151 **W**hat do you get when you cross a baby rabbit with a vegetable?

A bunion.

152 **A** grizzly bear walks into a bar and says to the bartender, 'I'll have a gin and . . . tonic.'

Bartender: *'What's with the big pause?'*

Bear: *'I don't know. My father had them, too.'*

153 **W**hy did the man cross a chicken with an octopus?

So everyone in his family could have a leg each.

154 **W**hat is white, lives in the Himalayas and lays eggs?

The Abominable Snow Chicken.

155 **H**ow do pigs get clean?

They go to the hogwash.

156 **W**hat happens when a chimpanzee sprains his ankle?

He gets a monkey wrench.

157 **W**hat happened to two frogs that caught the same bug at the same time?

They got tongue-tied.

158 **H**ow do you know when it's raining cats and dogs?

You step into a poodle.

159 **W**hy did the dinosaur cross the road?

Because there were no chickens.

160 **W**hat do you call a crazy chicken?

A cuckoo cluck.

161 **W**hat do you get if you cross Bambi with a ghost?

Bamboo.

162 **W**hy did the dinosaur not cross the road?

It was extinct.

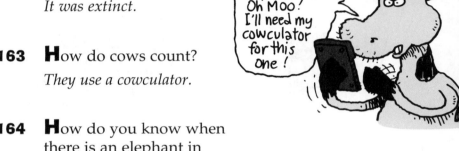

163 **H**ow do cows count?

They use a cowculator.

164 **H**ow do you know when there is an elephant in the fridge?

There are footprints in the butter.

165 **W**hat's grey and can't see well from either end?

A donkey with its eyes shut.

166 **W**hy are old dinosaur bones kept in a museum?

Because they can't find any new ones.

167 **W**hat's got six legs and can fly long distances?

Three swallows.

168 **W**hat do you get if you cross a pig with a zebra?

Striped sausages.

169 **D**id you hear about the monkey who left bits of his lunch all over the computer?

His dad went bananas.

170 **W**hat do you get if you cross a dinosaur with a werewolf?

Who knows, but I wouldn't want to be within a thousand miles of it when the moon is full!

171 **W**hy did the cat sit on the computer?

To keep an eye on the mouse.

172 **W**hen do kangaroos celebrate their birthdays?

During leap year.

173 **W**hat do baby swans dance to?

Cygnet-ure tunes.

174 **W**hat is a duck's favourite TV show?

The feather forecast.

175   **W**hat did the rabbit give his girlfriend when they got engaged?

A 24-carrot ring.

176   **W**hy don't baby birds smile?

Would you smile if your mother fed you worms all day?

177   **W**hat do you call a chicken that lays light bulbs?

A battery hen.

178   **W**hy do bears have fur coats?

Because they can't get plastic raincoats in their size!

179   **W**here is the hottest place in the jungle?

Under a gorilla.

180 **W**hat would you get if you crossed a hunting dog with a journalist?

A news hound.

181 **W**hat do you get if you cross a parrot with a shark?

A bird that will talk your ear off!

182 **D**octor, Doctor, I feel like a sheep.

That's baaaaaaaaaad!

183 **W**hat do you get if you cross an electric eel with a sponge?

Shock absorbers.

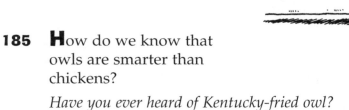

184 **W**hich birds steal the soap from the bath?

Robber ducks.

185 **H**ow do we know that owls are smarter than chickens?

Have you ever heard of Kentucky-fried owl?

186 **W**hen is a lion not a lion?

When he turns into his den.

187 **D**octor, Doctor, I think I'm a python.

You can't get round me just like that, you know!

188 **W**hat does an octopus wear when it's cold?

A coat of arms.

WASH DAY AT THE OCTOPUS' PLACE

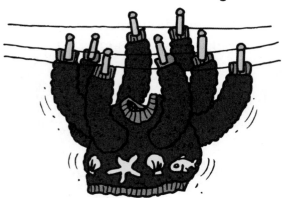

189 **W**hat's slimy, tastes of raspberry, is wobbly and lives in the sea?

A red jellyfish.

190 **H**ow do you know when a spider is cool?

It has its own website.

191 **N**ow you see it, now you don't. What could you be looking at?

A black cat walking over a zebra crossing!

192 **W**hat did the mouse say to the elephant?

Squeak.

SQUEAK

AAARHH

193 **W**hat bird tastes just like butter?

A stork.

194 **W**hat's the difference between a dark sky and an injured lion?

One pours with rain, the other roars with pain.

195 **W**hat did the croaking frog say to her friend?

I think I've got a person in my throat.

196 **W**hat did the termite say when she saw that her friends had completely eaten a chair?

'Wooden you know it!'

Your chair was delicious... Do you mind if I try the table?

197 **S**heep 1: *'Baa.'*

Sheep 2: *'I knew you were going to say that.'*

198 **W**hat are teenage giraffes told when they go on their first date?

No necking.

199 **W**hat did the boa constrictor say to its victim?

'I've got a crush on you.'

200 **W**hat disease do you have if you're allergic to horses?

Bronco-itis.

201 **W**hat do cats eat as a special treat?

Mice creams.

202 **W**hat do bees do with their honey?

They cell it.

203 **W**hat do bees use to communicate with each other?

Their cell phones.

204 **H**ow would you feel if you saw a dinosaur in your backyard?

Very old.

205 **W**hen did the last dinosaur die?

After the second-last dinosaur.

206 **W**hat do you cut a dinosaur bone with?

A dino-saw.

207 What do you get when you cross a dinosaur with a pig?

Jurassic Pork.

208 **W**hat do cows listen to?

Moosic.

209 **W**hat do you call a baby whale that never stops crying?

A little blubber.

210 **W**hat do you call a camel with no humps?

A horse.

211 **W**hy do elephants never get rich?

Because they work for peanuts.

212 **W**hat did the 100 kilo parrot say?

'Polly want a cracker, NOW!'

213 **D**id you hear
about the duck
decorator?

*He papered over
the quacks.*

214 **W**hat did one
bee say to her
nosy neighbour
bee?

*'Mind your own
bees' nest!'*

215 **W**hat do you do with a mouse that squeaks?

You oil him.

216 **H**ow does a jellyfish race start?

Get set.

217 What do you call a cat who lives in a hospital?

A first aid kit.

218 What do you call a Chinese cat that spies through windows?

A Peking Tom.

219 What do you get when you cross a bear with a cow?

Winnie the Moo.

220 What do you get when you cross a black bird with a madman?

A raven lunatic.

221 What do you get when you cross a chicken with a cement mixer?

A bricklayer.

222 What do you get when you cross a cow with a clairvoyant?

A message from the udder side.

223 **W**hat do you get when you cross a shark with a crocodile and a Tyrannosauraus rex?

I don't know, but don't take it swimming.

224 **W**hat do you get when you cross a cow with a whale?

Mooby Dick.

225 **W**hat do you get if you cross a duck with a firework?

A fire-quacker.

226 **W**hat do you get when you cross a hare with a walking stick?

A hurry-cane (hurricane).

227 **W**hat do you get when you cross a kangaroo with a skyscraper?

A high jumper.

228 **W**hat do you get when you cross a mouse and a deer?

Mickey Moose.

229 **W**hat do you get when you cross a hippopotamus with someone who is always sick?

A hippochondriac.

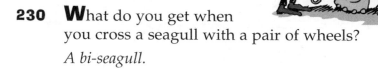

230 **W**hat do you get when you cross a seagull with a pair of wheels?

A bi-seagull.

231 **W**hat do you get when you cross a sheep with a radiator?

Central bleating.

232 **W**hat do you get when you cross an elephant with a bottle of rum?

Trunk and disorderly.

233 **W**hat do you get when you cross an elephant with a cake?

Crumbs.

234 **W**hat language do birds speak?

Pigeon English.

Someone suggested a game of 'HERE COMES THE LION' at Jumbo's 3rd Birthday party startling his 2 ton friends into a stampede.

235 **W**hat's as large as a horse but doesn't weigh anything?

Its shadow.

236 **H**ow do dinosaurs pay their bills?

With Tyrannosaurus cheques.

237 **H**ow do dinosaurs pass exams?

With extinction.

238 **W**hat do you get when you cross a dinosaur with explosives?

Dino-mite.

239 **W**hat do you get when you cross a Stegosaurus with a pig?

A porky spine.

240 **W**hat's the hardest part of making dinosaur stew?

Finding a pot big enough to hold the dinosaur.

241 **W**hat's the scariest dinosaur of all?

The Terrordactyl.

SCARY HEY?

The scariest thing in Prehistoric skies...
The Terrorsaurus

242 **W**here do dinosaurs go to the toilet?

In the dino-sewer.

243 **W**hich dinosaur does well in English exams?

Tyrannathesaurus rex.

244 **H**ow did Noah steer the Ark at night?

He switched on the floodlights.

After 40 days and 40 nights in this Ark with all these smelly animals...that looks like great land to me... THROW OUT THE ANCHOR!

245 **W**hy did the zookeeper refuse to work in the elephant enclosure?

Because the work kept piling up.

246 **W**hy do chickens watch TV?

For hentertainment.

247 **W**hy do frogs like beer?

Because it is made from hops.

248 **W**hat did Noah say as he was loading the animals?

'Now I herd everything.'

249 **W**hy don't cats shave?

Because they prefer Whiskas.

250 **W**hy is the letter 'T' important to a stick insect?

Because without it, it would be a sick insect.

251 **W**hy should you never fight an echidna?

Because she will always win on points.

252 **W**hy was the alligator called Kodak?

Because he was always snapping.

253 **W**hy did the chicken cross the road, roll in the mud and cross the road again?

Because it was a dirty double-crosser.

254 **W**hy did the chicken join the band?

Because it had drumsticks.

255 **W**hy did the fish cross the sea?

To get to the other tide.

256 **W**hy was the kangaroo mad at her children?

Because they were jumping on the bed.

257 **W**hy was the little bear spoilt?

Because he was panda'd to.

258 **W**hat do you get if you cross an elephant with a box of laxatives?

Out of the way.

259 **W**hy are dolphins clever?

Because they live in schools.

260 **W**hy can't frogs get life insurance?

Because they are always croaking.

261 **W**hy can't you have a conversation with a goat?

Because it always butts in.

262 **W**hich movie character do insects like best?

Bug Lightyear.

263 **W**hy are beavers so smart?

Because they gnaw everything.

264 **W**ho is the most feared animal of all?

Attila the Hen.

I never thought that little chick Attila would turn out to be such a wildgirl!

265 **W**hich TV show do cows never miss?

The moos.

266 **W**hich TV show do horses like best?

Neigh-bours.

Gold... coins... taxes... wives... Who needs them Just bring me BANANAS!

267 **W**ho is emperor of all mice?

Julius Cheeser.

268 **W**ho is the king of the monkeys?

Henry the Ape.

269 **W**hy can't you play a
practical joke on snakes?

Because they don't have a leg to pull.

270 **W**here would you
weigh a whale?

*At a whale-weigh
station.*

271 **W**hich animals are
best at maths?

*Rabbits, because they're
always multiplying.*

*Why YAKS are found only in the
highest mountains of the
Himalayas!*

272 **W**hich animal never stops
talking?

The yak.

273 **W**hich bird can lift the
heaviest weights?

The crane.

274 **W**hich bird never grows
up?

The minor bird.

275 **W**hich bird succeeds?

A budgie without teeth.

276 **W**hich hen lays the longest?

A dead one.

277 **W**hat do you give an elephant with diarrhoea?

Plenty of room.

278 **W**hat's the difference between a bird and a fly?

A bird can fly but a fly can't bird.

279 **W**hat's the difference between a buffalo and a bison?

You can't wash your hands in a buffalo.

280 **W**hat's the healthiest insect?

A vitamin bee.

281 **W**hen is a brown dog not a brown dog?

When it's a greyhound.

282 **W**hen is the best time to buy a canary?

When it's going cheap.

283 **W**here did the cow go for its holiday?
Moo Zealand.

284 **W**here do baby elephants come from?
Very big storks.

285 **W**here do baby monkeys sleep?
In an apricot.

286 **W**here do chickens go to die?
To oven.

287 **W**here did Noah keep the bees?
In the ark hives.

288 **W**here do cows go for entertainment?
The moovies.

289 **W**here do monkeys cook their dinner?
Under the gorilla.

Food for Thought

290 **W**hat can you serve, but never eat?

A tennis ball.

291 **W**hat vegetable goes well with jacket potatoes?

Button mushrooms.

292 **W**hat jam can't you eat?

A traffic jam!

293 **W**hat is a goalkeeper's favourite snack?

Beans on post!

294 **W**hat do you get when you cross an orange with a squash court?

Orange squash.

295 **W**hat happened when there was a fight in the fish and chip shop?

Two fish got battered.

296 **W**hat's the difference between a young lady and a fresh loaf?

One is a well-bred maid and the other is well-made bread.

297 **W**hat did one tomato say to the other that was behind?

Ketchup!

Where all the slow tomatoes end up.

TOMATO KETCHUP

298 **W**hat is the difference between a hungry person and a greedy person?

One longs to eat, and the other eats too long.

299 **W**hat do bees do if they want to catch public transport?

Wait at a buzz stop.

300 **W**hat is the difference between broccoli and boogers?

Kids don't like to eat broccoli!

301 **W**hat's green and short and goes camping?

A boy sprout.

302 **W**hat's the difference between a nightwatchman and a butcher?

One stays awake and the other weighs a steak!

303 **W**hy did the farmer plough his field with a steamroller?

He wanted to grow mashed potatoes.

304 What do you get if you cross Frankenstein with a hot dog?

Frankenfurterstein.

305 What should you take if a monster invites you to dinner?

Someone who can't run as fast as you.

306 **W**hat did the dragon say when he saw St George in his shining armour?

'Oh no! Not more tinned food!'

JUST HEAT and SERVE ...umm that's quick and easy!

TINNED KNIGHT

307 **W**hen the cannibal crossed the Pacific on a cruise ship, he told the waiter to take the menu away and bring him the passenger list!

308 **W**here do ants eat?

A restaur-ant.

309 **W**hat do you do if your chicken feels sick?

Give her an eggs-ray.

310 **W**hy did the monster eat the light bulb?

He wanted some light refreshment.

311 **M**other: *'I told you not to eat cake before supper.'*

Son: *'But it's part of my homework – see – if you take an eighth of a cake from a whole cake, how much is left?'*

312 **L**ucy: *'If you eat any more ice cream, you'll burst.'*

Lindy: *'Okay – pass the ice cream and duck.'*

313 **W**hat does a Yeti eat for dinner?

An ice-burger.

314 **K**nock knock.

Who's there?

Bach!

Bach who?

Bach of chips!

315 **K**nock knock.
Who's there?
Bacon!
Bacon who?
Bacon a cake for your birthday!

316 **A** man went into a cafe and ordered two slices of apple pie with four scoops of ice cream, covered with lashings of raspberry sauce and piles of chopped nuts.

'Would you like a cherry on top?' asked the waitress.

'No thanks,' said the man. *'I'm on a diet.'*

317 **W**hat do vultures always have for dinner?
Leftovers.

318 **H**ow do you make a cream puff?
Make it run around the block.

319 **W**hat is a termite's favourite breakfast?

Oak-meal.

320 **W**hy did the lazy boy get a job in a bakery?

Because he wanted a good loaf!

321 **K**nock knock.

Who's there?

Beef!

Beef who?

Bee fair now!

322 **D**octor, Doctor, I keep getting a pain in the eye when I drink coffee.

Have you tried taking the spoon out of the cup before you drink?

323 **K**nock knock.

Who's there?

Brie!

Brie who?

Brie me my supper!

324 **K**nock knock.

Who's there?

Butcher!

Butcher who?

Butcher arms around me!

325 **H**ave you ever seen a man-eating tiger?

No, but in a restaurant next door I once saw a man eating chicken . . .

326 **W**aiter, how did this fly get in my soup?

I guess it flew.

327 **W**aiter, I can't eat this meal. Fetch me the manager.

It's no use. He won't eat it either.

328 **W**aiter, do you have frogs' legs?

Yes sir.

Then hop to the kitchen and fetch me a steak.

Gee... I'm glad I always carry a spare sausage behind my ear to write with.

329 When the wally's co-worker asked why he had a sausage stuck behind his ear, he replied, *'Oh – I must have eaten my pencil for lunch!'*

330 How do you make a banana split?

Cut it in half.

331 How do you make a French fry?

Leave him in the sun.

My left thumb thinks it's Cream of Chicken ...my right thinks it's Pumpkin!

332 How do you make a fruit punch?

Give it boxing lessons.

333 *'Your finger is in my bowl of soup!'* said the man.

'Don't worry,' said the wally waiter. *'The soup isn't hot.'*

334 What happened to the male bee who fell in love?

He got stuck on his honey.

335 What's the best way to face a timid mouse?

Lie down in front of its mouse hole and cover your nose with cheese spread!

336 **W**here do sharks shop?

The fish market.

337 **W**hat do fishermen eat at Easter?

Oyster eggs.

338 **W**hat's a lawyer's favourite dessert?

Suet.

339 **W**hat's rhubarb?

Embarrassed celery.

340 **D**octor, Doctor, should I surf the Internet on an empty stomach?

No, you should do it on a computer.

341 **H**ow do you start a race between two rice puddings?

Sago.

342 **W**hat did the mayonnaise say to the fridge?

'Close the door, I'm dressing.'

343 **D**octor, Doctor, I feel like an apple.

We must get to the core of this!

344 '**W**illiam,' shouted his mum. *'There were two pieces of cake in that pantry last night, and now there's only one. How do you explain that?'*

'It was dark in the pantry,' said William. *'And I didn't see the second piece!'*

345 **W**aiter there's a fly in my soup.
Well you did order fly soup, ma'am.

346 **W**aiter, what kind of soup is this?
Bean soup.

I don't care what it's been. What is it now?

347 **C**harley: *'My cat likes to drink lemonade.'*

Lenny: *'Golly, he sure must be a sourpuss!'*

348 **D**ick and Jane were arguing over the breakfast table.
'Oh, you're so stupid!' shouted Dick.
'Dick!' said their father. *'That's quite enough! Now say you're sorry.'*
'Okay,' said Dick. *'Jane, I'm sorry you're stupid.'*

349 Johnny collected lots of money from trick-or-treating and he went to the store to buy some chocolate.

'*You should give that money to charity,*' said the shopkeeper.

'*No thanks,*' replied Johnny. '*I'll buy the chocolate – you give the money to charity!*'

350 What kind of sharks never eat women?

Man-eating sharks.

That's alright... I don't like the taste of you either.'

351 How do you make a swiss roll?

Push him down a hill.

352 How do you make an apple crumble?

Smash it with a mallet.

353 Two cannibals were having lunch.

'*Your girlfriend makes a great soup,*' said one to the other.

'*Yes!*' agreed the first. '*But I'm going to miss her!*'

So who's in your soup?

I don't know...but it tastes like they were wearing Cologne

354 **H**ow do you make an egg laugh?

Tell it a yolk.

355 **W**hy did the girl feed money to her cow?

Because she wanted to get rich milk.

356 **W**hy did the girl put a chicken in a tub of hot water?

Because she wanted the chicken to lay hard-boiled eggs!

357 **'I**t's a pity you've gone on a hunger strike,' said the convict's girlfriend on visiting day.

'Why?' asked the convict.

'Because I've put a file in your cake!'

Oh come on...
I can handle
a hair...or even
half a cockroach
in a cake...
but not a FILE!

20508

358 **G**irl: *'How much is a soft drink?'*

Waitress: *'Fifty cents.'*

Girl: *'How much is a refill?'*

Waitress: *'The first is free.'*

Girl: *'Well then, I'll have a refill.'*

359 **K**nock knock.

Who's there?

Cantaloupe!

Cantaloupe who?

Cantaloupe with you tonight!

360 **W**hat do you call an egg in the jungle?

An eggsplorer.

361 **K**nock knock.

Who's there?

Zubin!

Zubin who?

Zubin eating garlic again!

If an egg in the jungle is called an EGGSPLORER, What do you call an egg under an explorer's boot?

SQUASHED!

362 **A**my: *'Did you find your cat?'*

Karen: *'Yes, he was in the refrigerator.'*

Amy: *'Goodness, is he okay?'*

Karen: *'He's more than okay – he's a cool cat!'*

363 **W**aiter, I'd like burnt steak and soggy chips with a grimy, bitter salad.

I'm afraid the chef won't cook that for you, sir.

Why not? He did yesterday.

364 **W**hich cheese is made backwards?

Edam.

365 **W**hat vegetable can you play snooker with?

A cue-cumber.

366 **H**ow does Dracula eat his food?

In bite sized pieces.

367 **T**he cruise-ship passenger was feeling really seasick, when the waiter asked if he'd like some lunch.

'No thanks,' he replied. 'Just throw it over the side and save me the trouble.'

368 **W**hat's small, round, white and giggles?

A tickled onion.

369 **W**hat do nudists like to eat best?

Skinless sausages.

370 **W**hy did the tomato blush?

Because it saw the salad dressing.

371 **W**hat do lions say before they go out hunting for food?

Let us prey.

372 **W**hat's a lion's favourite food?

Baked beings.

373 **W**hy do gingerbread men wear trousers?

Because they have crummy legs.

374 **A** mushroom walks into a bar and says to the bartender, *'Get me a drink!'*

But the bartender refuses.

The mushroom says, *'Why not? I'm a fun-gi!'*

We don't serve fungus at this bar! Besides... you're dropping spores all over the counter!

375 **W**hy do watermelons get married?

Because they can't-elope.

On account of the high crime rate and being previously assaulted... the pack of peanuts opted for a quiet night in.

376 **W**hy does steak taste better in space?

Because it is meteor.

377 **W**hy don't nuts go out at night?

Because they don't want to be assaulted.

378 **W**hat do you get when you cross an overheating Apple computer with fast food?

A Big Mac and fries.

379 **W**aiter, there's a cockroach in my soup.

Sorry sir, we're all out of flies.

380 **W**hat are monsters' favourite lunches?

Shepherd's pie and ploughman's lunch.

381 **H**ow does Frankenstein eat?

He bolts his food down.

382 **K**nock knock.

Who's there?

U-8!

U-8 who?

U-8 my lunch!

True Colours

383 **W**hat's green, covered in custard and sad?

Apple grumble.

384 **W**hat's red on the outside and green inside?

A dinosaur wearing red pyjamas.

385 **B**oy monster: *'You've got a face like a million dollars.'*
Girl monster: *'Have I really?'*
Boy monster: *'Sure, it's green and wrinkly!'*

386 **B**oy: *'Dad there's a black cat in the dining room!'*
Dad: *'That's okay son, black cats are lucky.'*
Son: *'This one is – he's eaten your dinner!'*

387 **T**hree girls walked into a barber shop. Two had blonde hair and one had green hair. The barber asked the blondes, *'How did you get to be blonde?'*

'Oh, it's natural,' they replied.

The barber asked the other girl, *'How did your hair become green?'*

She replied – (now put your hand on your nose and rub up to your hair . . .)

> You know... you can get the same look just by using green mousse.

388 **W**hat do you do with a blue monster?

Try to cheer him up a bit.

Obviously radical babies

389 **W**hy do we dress baby girls in pink and baby boys in blue?

Because babies can't dress themselves.

390 **V**isitor: *'You're very quiet, Louise.'*

Louise: *'Well, my mum gave me a dollar not to say anything about your red nose.'*

391 **W**hat is red, sweet and bites people?

A jampire!

392 If everyone bought a white car, what would we have?

A white carnation.

393 'Is that the computer help line? Every time I log on to the Seven Dwarves website, my computer screen goes snow white . . .'

394 What do you get if you cross a teacher and a traffic warden?

Someone who gives you 500 double yellow lines for being late.

395 What's the tallest yellow flower in the world?

A giraffodil.

396 Why did the monster paint himself in rainbow coloured stripes?

He wanted to hide in a pencil case.

397 What's black and white and red all over?

A sunburned zebra.

398 What's green and hard?

A frog that lifts weights.

399 What's red and white?

Pink.

400 Who steals from her grandma's house?

Little Red Robin Hood.

401 What colour is a hiccup?

Burple.

402 What's red, white and brown and travels faster than the speed of sound?

An astronaut's ham and tomato sandwich.

403 What's green and pecks on trees?

Woody Wood Pickle.

404 **W**hat don't zombies wear on boat trips?

Life jackets.

405 **W**hat's green and sings?

Elvis Parsley.

406 **W**hat's green and slimy and hangs from trees?

Giraffe boogie.

On this tour of the African Plain you need to keep your eyes peeled for lions in long grass... scorpions under rocks... stampeding elephants... herds of wild wildebeasts... and of course Giraffe boogie in trees!

407 **W**hat's yellow and square?

A tomato in disguise.

408 **K**nock knock.

Who's there?

Beezer.

Beezer who?

Beezer black and yellow and make honey.

409 **W**hat goes in pink and comes out blue?

A swimmer on a cold day!

410 **W**hat's black and white and rolls down a hill?

A penguin.

411 **W**hat's black and white and laughs?

The penguin who pushed the other one.

412 **W**hat's big and white and can't jump over a fence?

A fridge.

413 **W**hich king was purple and had many wives?

King Henry the Grape.

414 **W**hat's purple, 5000 years old and 400 kilometres long?

The Grape Wall of China.

415 **W**hat's grey, has four legs and a trunk?

A mouse going on holiday.

416 What's thick and black and picks its nose?

Crude oil.

417 How many clothing shop assistants does it take to change a light bulb?

Three, one to change it, one to say how well it fits and one to say that the colour is perfect.

Rude and Crude

418 You're such a bad cook, even the maggots get takeaway.

419 Your family is so weird, when the doorbell rings your sister has to shout out 'Ding, dong.'

420 You are as useless as a screen door on a submarine.

421 With you here, your village must be missing its idiot.

Come back here little fella... Don't go wandering off... you're the only mind I've got!

422 Don't let your mind wander – it's too little to be let out alone.

423 **S**tatistics say that one in three people is wacky.

So check your friends and if two of them seem okay, you're the one . . .

424 **H**ere's 50 cents. Call all your friends and bring me back the change.

425 **Y**our dog is so slow, he brings in last week's newspaper.

426 **T**urn the other cheek. On second thoughts, don't. The view is just as ugly on that side.

427 You're not as stupid as you look. That would be impossible.

428 I'd leave you with one thought if you had somewhere to put it.

429 Your feet are so smelly, your shoes refuse to come out of the closet.

The other shoes in the wardrobe could stand the smell no longer... so the stinky sandshoes were shown the door...

430 If it's true that opposites attract, you'll meet someone who is good-looking, intelligent and cultured.

431 Everyone has the right to be ugly, but you abused the privilege.

432 She's so ugly, when a wasp stings her, it has to shut its eyes!

I'm not that desperate to sting someone!

433 If someone offered you a penny for your thoughts, they'd expect some change.

434 You're dark and handsome. When it's dark, you're handsome.

435 Last time I saw someone as ugly as you, I had to pay admission.

436 As an outsider, what do you think of the human race?

437 Instead of drinking from the fountain of knowledge, you just gargled.

438 They say that truth is stranger than fiction. And you're the proof.

439 I'll never forget the first time we met – although I keep trying.

440 **S**omeone told me you're not fit to live with pigs but I stuck up for you and said you were.

441 **Y**ou're so boring, you won't even talk to yourself.

442 **Y**ou're so ugly, the only dates you get are on a calendar.

443 **Y**ou're so ugly you have to trick or treat over the phone.

444 **Y**ou're growing on me – like a wart.

445 '**D**addy, can I have another glass of water, please?'

'Okay, but that's the twelfth one I've given you tonight.'

'Yes I know, but the house is still on fire.'

446 '**C**an *I go swimming now, Mum?'* asked the child.

'No – there are sharks at this beach,' said his mother.

'Dad's swimming!'

Yes, he's got a million dollars life insurance . . .'

447 **G**eorge is the type of boy that his mother doesn't want him to hang around with . . .

448 **D**id you hear about the two fat men who ran a marathon?

One ran in short bursts, the other ran in burst shorts.

449 **A** woman woke her husband in the middle of the night.

'There's a burglar in the kitchen eating the cake I made this morning!' she said.

'Who should I call?' asked her husband. *'The police or an ambulance?'*

450 **M**y cousin spent heaps on deodorant, until he found out people just didn't like him . . .

ERRRRR . . . it smells like something's died round here.

451 **D**id you hear about the two bodies cremated at the same time?

It was a dead heat.

452 **D**id you hear about the dentist who became a brain surgeon?

His drill slipped.

453 **W**hat's the difference between a peeping Tom and someone who's just got out of the bath?

One is rude and nosey. The other is nude and rosey!

454 **T**here's no point in telling some people a joke with a double meaning.

They wouldn't understand either of them!

455 Three guys, Shutup, Manners and Poop, drove too fast and Poop fell out of the car.

ERR...PHEW! What stinks?

I think it's POOP

Shutup went to the police station, where the policeman asked, *'What's your name?'*

'Shutup,' he answered.

'Hey – where are your manners!' the policeman exclaimed.

Shutup replied, *'Outside on the road, scrapin' up Poop!'*

456 As he was walking along a street, the minister saw a little girl trying to reach a high door knocker. Anxious to help, he went over to her. *'Let me do it, dear,'* he said, rapping the knocker.

'Thanks,' said the little girl. *'Now run like heck!'*

457 Why did the female frog lay eggs?

Because her husband spawned her affections.

458 Uncle Herbert noticed that his nephew Johnny was watching him all the time.

'Why are you always looking at me?' he asked.

'I was just wondering when you were going to do your trick,' replied Johnny.

'What trick?' asked Uncle Herbert.

'Well, Mum says you eat like a horse...'

459 **A** man out for a walk came across a little boy pulling his cat's tail.

'Hey you!' he shouted. *'Don't pull the cat's tail!'*

'I'm not pulling,' replied the boy. *'I'm only holding on – the cat's doing the pulling. . .'*

460 **M**y dad once stopped a man ill-treating a donkey.

It was a case of brotherly love. . .

461 **W**hat's three feet tall, has twelve fingers, three eyes and wears sunglasses?

A monster on summer vacation.

462 **W**hen the man was run over by a steamroller, what was proved?

That he had lots of guts.

The next scene is just too ugly to draw...'

463 **W**hy shouldn't you sleep on trains?

They run over sleepers!

464 **W**hat do you call a one-legged woman?

Eileen!

465 **R**oger was in a full bus when a fat lady opposite said to him, *'If you were a gentleman, you'd stand up and let someone else sit down.'* *'And if you were a lady,'* Roger replied, *'you'd stand up and let four people sit down!'*

466 **A** woman was facing court, charged with wounding her husband.

'You're very lucky you're not facing a murder charge – why did you stab him over a hundred times?' asked the judge.

'I didn't know how to turn off the electric carving knife,' she replied.

467 **W**hat is the smelliest game in the world?

Ping pong!

World of Sport

468 **W**hat has 75 pairs of sneakers, a ball and two hoops?

A centipede basketball team.

469 **W**hy didn't the wally goalkeeper catch the ball?

He thought that's what the net was for.

Hey...you'll have to do that again...I wasn't ready.'

470 **'I** can't see us ever finishing this tenpin bowling game.'

'Why is that?'

'Every time I knock all the pins down, someone calls everyone out on strike!'

471 **H**ow many soccer players does it take to change a light bulb?

Eleven, one to change it, the others to jump about, hugging and kissing him.

472 **W**hy aren't football stadiums built in outer space?

Because there is no atmosphere!

473 **W**hich goalkeeper can jump higher than a crossbar?

All of them – a crossbar can't jump!

474 **W**hat's a pig's favourite ballet?

Swine Lake.

475 **W**here do footballers dance?

At a football!

476 **W**hy did the golfer wear two pairs of trousers?

In case he got a hole in one.

477 **W**hat job does Dracula have with the Transylvanian baseball team?

He looks after the bats.

478 **W**hat do you call a cat that plays football?

Puss in boots.

479 **W**hat lights up a football stadium?

A football game!

480 **W**hy do football coaches bring suitcases along to away games?

So that they can pack the defence!

481 If you have a referee in football, what do you have in bowls?

Cornflakes!

482 How do hens encourage their football teams?

They egg them on!

483 How do you start a doll's race?

Ready, Teddy, Go!

FINISH

It's a tie.

484 Who won the race between two balls of string?

They were tied!

485 How did the basketball court get wet?

The players dribbled all over it!

Forget the cricket or football matches. ...I'd rather just sit around chewing a leaf

486 Why don't grasshoppers go to football matches?

They prefer cricket matches!

487 Why didn't the dog want to play football?

It was a boxer!

488 **W**hen fish play football, who is the captain?
The team's kipper!

489 **H**ow do you stop squirrels playing football in the garden?
Hide the ball, it drives them nuts!

490 **W**hy should you be careful when playing against a team of big cats?
They might be cheetahs!

491 **N**ame a tennis player's favourite city.
Volley Wood!

492 **W**here do football directors go when they are sick of the game?
The bored room!

493 **W**hat's a vampire's favourite sport?
Batminton.

494 **W**hat do vampire footballers have at half time?
Blood oranges.

495 **C**oach: *'I thought I told you to lose weight. What happened to your three-week diet?'*

Player: *'I finished it in three days!'*

496 **W**hat do you get when you cross a skunk with a table-tennis ball?

Ping pong.

497 **H**ow many baseball players does it take to change a light bulb?

Two, one to change it, the other to signal which way to do it.

498 **W**hat do you get when you cross a plumber with a ballerina?

A tap dancer.

499 **C**oach: *'Our new player cost ten million. I call him our wonder player.'*

Fan: *'Why's that?'*

Coach: *'Every time he plays, I wonder why I bothered to buy him!'*

500 **C**oach: *'I'll give you $100 a week to start with, and $500 a week in a year's time.'*

Young player: *'See you in a year!'*

501 **W**hat did the football player say when he accidentally burped during the game?

'Sorry, it was a freak hic!'

502 **W**hat part of a basketball stadium is never the same?

The changing rooms!

503 **W**hat happens when an athlete gets angry with his computer?

He becomes a floppy diskus thrower.

504 **W**here do old bowling balls end up?

In the gutter!

505 **W**hy do artists never win when they play basketball?

They keep drawing!

506 **W**hat are Brazilian fanatics called?

Brazil nuts!

507 **W**hat did they call Dracula when he won the premiership?

The Champire!

508 **W**hy does someone who runs marathons make a good student?

Because education pays off in the long run!

509 **W**hat stories are told by basketball players?

Tall stories!

510 **W**hy did the footballer take a piece of rope onto the pitch?

He was the skipper!

511 **W**hat baseball position did the boy with no arms or legs play?

Home base.

512 **W**hat wears nine gloves, 18 shoes and a mask?

A baseball team.

513 **W**hy was the struggling manager seen shaking the club cat?

To see if there was any money in the kitty!

Music to My Ears

514 **W**hy did the singer climb a ladder?

To reach the high notes.

515 **H**ow many country music singers does it take to change a light bulb?

Two, one to change it, the other to sing about how heartbroken he is that the old one is finished.

516 **D**id you hear about the wally burglar?

He robbed a music store and stole the lute.

517 What type of music do mummies like best?

Ragtime.

518 What's a skeleton's favourite musical instrument?

A trom-bone.

519 'My brother's been practising the violin for ten years.'

'Is he any good?'

'No, it was nine years before he found out he wasn't supposed to blow!'

520 **K**nock knock.
Who's there?
Cecil.
Cecil who?
Cecil have music wherever she goes.

521 **W**hat do you call a guy who hangs around musicians?
A drummer.

522 **W**hat type of music do zombies like best?
Soul music.

523 **W**hat sort of music is played most in the jungle?
Snake, rattle and roll.

524 **W**hat type of music do geologists like best?
Rock.

525 **W**hy did the monster eat his music teacher?
His Bach was worse than his bite.

526 **W**hat was Pavarotti before he was a tenor?
A niner.

527 **W**hat do you call a small Indian guitar?
A baby sitar.

528 **W**here do musicians live?
In A flat.

529 **'T**his piece of music is haunting.'
'That's because you're murdering it.'

530 **H**ow do you make a bandstand?
Take away their chairs.

The painful murder of the "1812 Overture"

531 **'I** played Beethoven last night.'
'Who won?'

532 **W**hy did the footballer hold his boot to his ear?
Because he liked sole music!

533 **'W**hat shall I sing next?'

'Do you know "Bridge Over Troubled Waters?"'

'Yes.'

'Then go and jump off it.'

534 **W**hat do Eskimos sing at birthday parties?

'Freeze a Jolly Good Fellow.'

535 **W**hat does a musician take to the supermarket?

A Chopin Lizst.

536 **'O**ur Jackie learnt to play the violin in no time at all.'

'So I can hear.'

537 **W**hat instrument does a fisherman play?

A cast-a-net.

538 **W**hy couldn't the composer be found?

Because he was Haydn.

539 **W**hy was the musician in prison?

Because he was always getting into treble.

540 **W**hat kind of song can you sing in the car?

A cartoon (car tune)!

541 **W**here do musical frogs perform?

At the Hopera House.

Dumb and Dumber

542 You're so dumb, when you eat M&Ms, you throw out the Ws.

543 You're so ugly, when you enter a room, the mice jump on chairs.

Yep...that's right... It's a new mobile phone that has enough cable to reach just about anywhere!

544 You're so dumb, you took your mobile phone back to the shop because it came without a cord.

545 You're so dumb, it takes you an hour to cook one-minute noodles.

546 You're so dumb, you think the English Channel is a British TV station.

547 Did you hear what Dumb Donald did when he offered to paint the garage for his dad?

The instructions said put on three coats – so he put on his jacket, his raincoat and his overcoat!

548 My girlfriend talks so much that when she goes on vacation, she has to spread suntan lotion on her tongue!

549 Little Susie stood in the department store near the escalator, watching the moving handrail.

'Something wrong, little girl?' asked the security guard.

'Nope,' replied Susie. *'I'm just waiting for my chewing gum to come back.'*

550 **E**mma: *'What a cool pair of odd socks you have on, Jill.'*
Jill: *'Yes, and I have another pair just like it at home.'*

551 **D**ad: *'Don't be selfish. Let your brother use the sled half the time.'*
Son: *'I do, Dad. I use it going down the hill and he gets to use it coming up the hill!'*

552 **W**hy did the lion feel sick after he'd eaten the priest?

Because it's hard to keep a good man down.

553 **Y**ou're so dumb, when you went to the mind reader they couldn't find anything to read.

554 '**D**ad, can you write in the dark?'

'*I suppose so.*'

'Good. Can you sign my report card, please?'

555 '**M**um, I'm not going to school today.'

'*Why not?*'

'Because it's Sunday.'

556 **M**y big brother is such an idiot. The other day I saw him hitting himself over the head with a hammer.

He was trying to make his head swell, so his hat wouldn't fall over his eyes!

An ILL-FITTING HAT? I've got the perfect solution for an ill-fitting hat!

557 **W**hy did Silly Sue throw her guitar away?

Because it had a hole in the middle.

558 **A** man whose son had just passed his driving test came home one evening and found that the boy had driven into the living room.

'*How did you manage that?*' he fumed.

'*Quite simple, Dad,*' said the boy. '*I just came in through the kitchen and turned left.*'

559 '**W**hy are you crying, Ted?' asked his mum.

'*Because my new sneakers hurt,*' Ted replied.

'That's because you've put them on the wrong feet.'

'*But they're the only feet I have!*'

560 '**M**um, Mum, Dad's broken my computer!'

'*How did he do that?*'

'I dropped it on his head!'

561 **D**id you hear about my brother?

He saw a moose's head hanging on a wall and went into the next room to find the rest of it!

562 **A** boy was staying in an old house, and in the middle of the night, he met a ghost.

'*I've been walking these corridors for 300 years,*' said the ghost.

'*In that case, can you tell me where the bathroom is?*' asked the boy.

563 First witch: *'I took my son to the zoo yesterday.'*
Second witch: *'Really? Did they keep him?'*

564 Did you hear about the farmer's boy who hated the country?
He went to the big city and got a job as a shoeshine boy, and so the farmer made hay while the sun shone.

565 Mum: *'How can you practise your trumpet and listen to the radio at the same time?'*
Son: *'Easy, I have two ears!'*

566 'Mum,' Richard yelled from the kitchen. *'You know that dish you were always worried I'd break?'*
'Yes dear, what about it?' said his mum.
'Well . . . your worries are over.'

567 'Mum, there's a man at the door collecting for the Old Folks' Home,' said the little boy. *'Shall I give him Grandma?'*

Mum won't be too mad.... It's only broken into 3 big bits.

568 Two girls were having lunch in the school yard. One had an apple, and the other said, *'Watch out for worms, won't you!'*
The first girl replied, *'Why should I? They can watch out for themselves!'*

569 **W**hat do you call a top girl-group made up of nits?

The Lice Girls!

570 **W**hy did the boy wear a life jacket in bed?

Because he slept on a waterbed.

571 **J**ane: *'Do you like me?'*

Wayne: *'As girls go, you're fine . . . and the sooner you go, the better!'*

572 **D**ad was taking Danny around the museum, when they came across a magnificent stuffed lion in a case.

'Dad,' asked a puzzled Danny. *'How did they shoot the lion without breaking the glass?'*

573 Boy: *'Grandpa, do you know how to croak?'*

Grandpa: *'No, I don't. Why?'*

Boy: *'Because Daddy says he'll be a rich man when you do!'*

574 You're so slow, you can't even catch your breath.

575 John: *'Have you noticed your mother smells a bit funny these days?'*

Will: *'No. Why?'*

John: *'Well, your sister told me she was giving her a bottle of toilet water for her birthday!'*

576 You're so dumb, when your teacher said she wanted you to get ahead, she really meant 'a head'.

577 *'Mum, can I please change my name right now?'* asked Ben.

'Why would you want to do that, dear?' asked his mum.

'Because Dad says he's going to spank me, as sure as my name's Benjamin!'

578 What does a
wally pour over
his meat?

Thick gravy.

579 George knocked on the door of his friend's house.
When his friend's mother answered he asked, *'Can
Albert come out to play?'*

'No,' said Albert's mother. *'It's too cold.'*

'Well then,' said George, *'can his football come out to
play?'*

580 'William, I've been told you tried to put paint on
two boys at school,' said his dad.

'Yes Dad,' said William.

They're twins and I needed a way to tell them apart!'